Twenty Two
Brilliant British Birds

*A cheerful account of some of the
remarkable talents and personalities of a
selection of our favourite British birds*

Guy Riches

Illustrations by Mike Langman

For

Connie, Isla and Eliza

"Be as a bird perched on a frail branch that she feels bending beneath her, still she sings away all the same, knowing she has wings."

Victor Hugo

"I think we consider too much the good luck of the early bird and not enough the bad luck of the early worm."

Franklin D. Roosevelt

Publisher: Independent Publishing Network

Publication Date: 2020

Designed and printed in the UK by Short Run Press Ltd

ISBN: 9781838532529

Author: Guy Riches

Illustrations by Mike Langman

Please direct all enquiries to the author

twentytwobirdbooks@gmail.com

Twenty Two Bird Books are on Facebook.
Please follow us there and help to spread the word
through likes and shares

Contents

Introduction

The British Isles are home or sometime home to over three hundred different birds, large and small, fast and slow, silent and noisy, residents and visitors, seabirds and farmland birds, some that sing and some that squawk. They may nest in trees, on open ground, or perhaps on a cliff face. One colourful bird nests in a burrow, like a rabbit, and moos like a cow.

This book looks at Twenty Two Brilliant British Birds that we can all hope to see in any one year if we stay alert and are lucky enough to be in the right place at the right time. Many of these birds can be seen every day in our parks and gardens, and across our woods and farmland or on our seashores. While many may be fairly common, depending on the season, a few of these birds are much harder to find; special effort is required to track down a puffin, the barn owl can prove elusive and the source of the most famous of all the sounds of spring, the cuckoo, is these days a rare and precious joy.

Around half of all our British Isles birds live here all year round, being resident, while the other half are welcome visitors, or migrants, living with us for only part of the year either to breed during our warmer summer months or to escape the arctic north and frozen east in order to enjoy our milder maritime winters. Most of the twenty two birds on these pages can be seen all year round, but some we will only see in the spring and summer, others only in the autumn and winter.

Even amongst this small selection of birds we see a huge variation in size, weight and wingspan. The great tit is only half the size of a blackbird. A heron is ten times as tall as a robin. A gannet, which might be twenty five years old, is over two hundred times heavier than a goldfinch, similar to the weight difference between a swan and an elephant.

These twenty two birds all have distinctive personalities, appearance, habits and talents. They are all capable of remarkable individual behaviour, journeys and exploits. A knowledge of these few birds helps us to better appreciate the abundance of nature across our bountiful British Isles.

The Skylark

Many birds have names that reflect their character. The delightful skylark certainly seems to "lark around", ascending in stilted stages and later parachuting back to earth. They are found at all times of the year on and above areas of pasture and arable farmland. Seen alone or in pairs in the spring and summer they form small friendly flocks in winter, when we may see them quite close by over winter stubble.

In the spring and summer months you will hear the skylark's cheerful song well before you see this determined small bird, who seems at first invisible. They sing with hardly a pause for breath from an almost stationary position, floating high above. Only after a long search of the bright blue sky will you finally spot the tiny speck of the skylark, high overhead, singing his constant happy summer song.

This is the skylark's way of life in the spring and summer months and there is good reason for this behaviour. Some birds protect themselves by staying silent and well hidden. Male skylarks choose instead to proclaim their presence, singing loudly as a clear statement that they are the rulers of their territory. Or perhaps just drawing attention away from the female? She's carefully concealed on the ground directly below, shielding a precious clutch of eggs or a brood of chicks.

Seen where and when	All year round on and above arable fields and pasture
What it eats	Seeds and insects
Collective noun	An "exaltation" of skylarks
Lifespan	2-3 years on average, up to 10
Wingspan	12 inches or 33 cm
Length	8 inches or 20 cm
Latin name	*Alauda arvensis*
Alternative name	The Laverbrok or Lintwhite
Also look out for	Shorelarks, Woodlarks and Wagtails

The Invisible Bird

The Robin *(Robin Redbreast)*

Most birds are shy and nervous. They keep their distance, almost always taking flight if we get too close or if startled by the slightest noise or movement. Robins make it very clear indeed if they feel disturbed and demonstrate, for such a small bird, a surprisingly loud and angry *tic, tic, tic* alarm call, if seeing or sensing danger.

There are times, however, when the friendly garden robin seems to have very little fear of humans. Easily recognizable by their vivid red breast, both cock and hen robins will settle or perch and watch over us, sometimes just an arm's length away, as we weed a flower bed, rake leaves or dig vegetables. They know that when we disturb the ground we are likely at any time to reveal their favourite food – a big juicy worm. The seemingly sociable robin sees us as a useful friend and provider of the occasional easy meal.

Gardeners certainly love to see a robin and appreciate the plucky redbreast's company as well as their enchanting tuneful song. Unlike almost any other bird, robins sing all year round and sometimes even in the dark of the night.

One of the best known and best loved of all British birds the brave and determined little redbreasts are highly territorial, angrily confronting and chasing away any other robins that dare to stray into their home patch. It may well be the same resident robin that you see day after day in your garden and quite likely from one year to the next.

Seen where and when	All year round across gardens, woodland and farmland
What it eats	Worms, fruits, seeds and insects
Collective noun	A "blush" of robins
Lifespan	2-3 years on average, up to 8
Wingspan	9 inches or 22 cm
Length	5 inches or 14 cm
Latin name	*Erithacus rubecula*
Alternative name	Red Breast or Bobbie
Also look out for	Wrens, Dunnocks and Tits

The Gardener's Friend

The Song Thrush

All songbirds sing to some extent and their birdsong is very different to their warnings and "calls". Bird calls are usually a series of quickly repeated notes, as opposed to their more fluid and musical song. Birds call to one another as a warning or perhaps simply to keep in touch. Many of the birds that are not songbirds have very distinctive individual calls, such as the frequent *caaw caaw caaaaw* of the cranky crow.

It is usually the male songbird, or cock bird, that we hear singing as he tries to attract a mate or protects his territory. In the first light of morning in spring and summer we hear a symphony of many different birds all singing or calling at the same time, this choir of multitudes making up the magnificent dawn chorus.

We generally think of three garden birds as having the finest song; the robin, the blackbird and the song thrush. Sometimes it seems the song thrush never stops singing. Usually seen alone on a branch he sings the same set of notes two or three times over. Often one line of song, the same three notes, followed by another three note line and then back again to the first. Or sometimes just the same two or three notes repeated over and over again. It is a lovely clear and crisp if somewhat repetitive bird song, often heard all day long throughout the spring and early summer months.

We will frequently hear the song thrush making a very different sound, as they briskly bash a snail against a stone. *Tap, tap, tap,* we hear. *Tap, tap, tap,* until finally the shell is broken open to reveal the slimy inner snail, a favourite song thrush snack.

Seen where and when	All year round in gardens, parkland and woodland
What it eats	Preferably snails
Collective noun	A "rash" of thrushes
Lifespan	3-4 years on average, up to 10
Wingspan	14 inches or 34 cm
Length	9 inches or 23 cm
Latin name	*Turdus philomelos*
Alternative name	The Mavis Throttle or Whistling Dick
Also look out for	Mistle Thrush or "Storm Cock"

The Singing Superstar

The Fieldfare

As autumn turns to winter in late October it is already bitterly cold in Scandinavia and Russia where the freezing winter sets in with deadly speed. The fieldfare now decide to make the long journey south and west to escape that bitter arctic cold. Members of the thrush family, fieldfare are smaller than our resident mistle thrushes and slightly larger than the song thrush, with a noticeably longer tail.

The garrulous fieldfare rove around our fields and gardens in large cheerful flocks. Spilling from tree to tree they are almost always to be heard chatting happily away, often mingling with friendly flocks of starlings, and settling to feed over pasture or stubble. At a time of year when many other birds are mute or rarely heard the lively fieldfare are an uplifting sound on otherwise grey winter days.

They feed hungrily on the early winter berries where farmers have kindly not yet cut the great lines of hawthorn and blackthorn hedgerows. These berries provide vital sugary goodness for the birds, helping them to build their strength ahead of the shorter, colder days to come.

Fieldfare are easily identifiable by their near constant chatter and by their habit of flocking together, while our resident thrushes tend to be seen alone or in pairs. Along with blackbirds and starlings they are one of our most numerous winter visitors. In early spring they disappear, just as suddenly as they arrived, only a few days before being replaced in our skies by the first April swallows.

Seen where and when	Across open countryside from October to April
What it eats	Seeds, berries and insects
Collective noun	A simple "flock" of fieldfare
Lifespan	2-3 years on average, up to 12
Wingspan	16 inches or 40 cm
Length	10 inches or 25 cm
Latin name	*Turdus pilaris*
Alternative name	The Grey Thrush
Also look out for	Redwings and Bramblings

The Winter Thrush

The Jackdaw

Young jackdaws have strikingly bright blue eyes. But when the jackdaw is a year or so old the outer blueness fades to the more human like white of the adult bird.

These dark grey birds are the smallest member of the crow family and were once seen as a hungry, noisy nuisance. At one time their numbers were so great that Queen Elizabeth I put a bounty on their head, with landowners forced to pay a fee for every bird killed and presented.

Jackdaws are usually seen in cohesive and sociable flocks, giving the impression of working together as a team, if sometimes in the boisterous manner of crowd of ruffians. They are less rowdy and considerably less noisy than their cousins the rooks and more tightly knit, less independent, than their other "corvid" cousins the crows. All of these crow species will flock together, at times, in winter.

Like the magpie, jackdaws are sometimes seen as thieves. They are interested in shiny objects and may pick up and fly away with an item of interest. Jackdaws will commonly mob other larger birds if they feel threatened, ganging up on, for instance, a buzzard. They will harass the buzzard in the air, chasing and clashing until the bigger bird has had enough and moves away to escape the hooligan mob.

They are thought to be one of the most intelligent of all birds, exhibiting genuine problem solving skills. If we help an injured jackdaw it will sometimes become tame and can, like a parrot, learn to recognise individual human sounds and faces.

Seen where and when	Across gardens and countryside all year round
What it eats	Seeds, fruits, insects and carrion
Collective noun	A "clattering" of jackdaws
Lifespan	4-5 years on average, up to 15
Wingspan	27 inches or 70 cm
Length	13 inches or 34 cm
Latin name	*Corvus monedula*
Alternative name	The Jack! Or Cawdaw
Also look out for	Crows, Jays and Magpies

The Blue Eyed Bird

The Starling

In October and November our resident starling population is swelled dramatically by the arrival of millions of winter visitors. We will sometimes see tens of thousands of starlings flocking together. Like the fieldfare they migrate to us from the frozen wilds of Scandinavia and Russia, seeking out our milder winter weather.

At dusk in the late autumn and throughout the winter they swoop and swirl together in one brilliant tight and fast moving mass of aerial acrobatics, becoming a rolling ball of thousands of birds dancing across the evening sky. This famous display is called a "murmuration" and is one of the most awe inspiring sights in nature. With such large numbers of birds in one small area the display is noisy as well as visually spectacular and it is probably intended to scare away local predators before the starlings settle down to roost.

Starlings are enchanting, eccentric and charismatic. They are joyful, sociable, boisterous and busy. They chatter to one another in a chorus of charming whistles and dolphin like squeaks. They also mimic other birds, possibly just for the fun of it. They change colour through the seasons, their brown winter chest turning by spring to an iridescent purple green, below a vivid yellow beak.

Seen where and when	All over all year round, millions present in winter
What it eats	Corn, leatherjackets and other bugs and insects
Collective noun	A "chattering" of starlings, a murmuration in winter
Lifespan	4-5 years on average, up to 15
Wingspan	15 inches or 40 cm
Length	9 inches or 24 cm
Latin name	*Sturnus vulgaris*
Alternative name	The Stare or Speckled Stare
Also look out for	Knots in winter, in huge coastal flocks

The Mimic and Master of Magnificent Murmurations!

The Great Tit

Amongst the more plentiful blue tits seen feeding at a bird table you may also spot the similar but less common (black headed) coal tits and the slightly larger great tit. The male great tit has one very distinctive characteristic that sets this proud bird apart from all others; he announces the end of winter.

Great tits provide us with the very first indication that winter is drawing to a snuffling shuffling close and that the warmer brighter spring will soon be upon us. They are the first of all our birds to start to call in search of a mate and his distinctive repetitive plea could easily be mistaken for a squeaky bicycle pump.

It is the male great tit who moves from tree to tree announcing himself to the world with his loud squeaky call. Sometimes called the "teacher bird" because the squeaky bicycle pump sound usually comes in blasts of three and sounds a bit like a creaky "teacher, teacher, teacher"...

Because the great tit starts to call so very early in the year we may hear him some weeks before any other bird. By February and March you'll be sure to hear the blackbird's busy chatter, the song of the melodic robin and the determined thrush. But from January onwards it's the great tit's charismatic call that is most distinctive. It is the unmistakable sound of lengthening days and makes the go-getting great tit one of the easiest of all small birds to identify, by his determined squeaky call.

Seen where and when	Across gardens, woodland and open countryside
What it eats	Small fruits and berries, seeds and insects
Collective noun	A "banditry" of tits
Lifespan	3-5 years on average, up to 15
Wingspan	10 inches or 25 cm
Length	5 inches or 13 cm
Latin name	*Parus major*
Alternative name	The Black Headed Tomtit or Bee-Biter
Also look out for;	Blue Tits, Coal Tits and Long Tailed Tits

The Squeaky Bicycle Pump

The Cuckoo

Cuckoos arrive in the British Isles in late April and early May having made the long flight from southern Africa; a similar epic journey to that of the swifts and the swallows and many other of our summer visitors.

Of the hundred or more species of birds who migrate to us from Africa to breed and feed perhaps the best known are the swallow and the cuckoo. Swallows are commonly seen but rarely heard, they hardly sing or call though they chat happily in long lines on telephone wires as they flock together in September, ahead of their return flight south. The cuckoo on the other hand is very rarely seen but quite often heard. In our spring we might be lucky enough to hear his distinctive cuck-coo, cuck-coo call. It is one of the most distinctive sounds in nature and a famous sound of the arrival of spring.

The Cuckoo cheats other birds. The female cuckoo will lay her eggs in another bird's nest, the unwitting host bird often being a dunnock or a reed warbler. The cuckoo removes one of the other bird's eggs and replaces it with her own. Once hatched, the cuckoo chick soon pushed all the other eggs or chicks out of the nest.

The poor deceived host bird now treats the lone cuckoo chick as her own and feeds and raises the imposter, despite the fact that within a few weeks the cuckoo fledgling may be more than twice her size. The cunning cuckoo has cheated the other bird into feeding and rearing her charlatan chick, and will repeat this trick across a dozen different nests throughout the spring.

Seen where and when	April to August across open countryside
What it eats	Insects and hairy caterpillars
Collective noun	An "asylum" of cuckoos
Lifespan	3-4 years on average, up to 6 years
Wingspan	24 inches or 60 cm
Length	14 inches or 35 cm
Latin name	*Cuculus canorus*
Alternative name	The Cog or Tittling
Also look out for	Swallows and Swifts

The Cheat!

The Blackbird

The blackbird is a noisy evening chatterbox, a numerous and common bird with very uncommon musical talent. Many people's favourite, the blackbird's song is one of the loveliest of all our sounds of nature. They sing from a prominent post or perch, often after rain, and in winter will sometimes sing very quietly, to themselves, hidden away in the undergrowth.

There are some five million resident blackbirds in the British Isles, meaning you are never far from one of these delightful busy birds. They are our most common breeding songbird. You will find them in most gardens and across all parks and farmland. Female blackbirds, the hen birds, are not black but darkling brown.

Ten million or more blackbirds join our resident population every winter, escaping the colder climates of their more northern and easterly breeding grounds. These winter visitors are almost exclusively the yellow beaked cock birds, the sensible hen birds seemingly seeking warmer weather further south.

Blackbirds are enthusiastic participants in the dawn chorus, but also perform a more exclusive blackbird dominated evening chorus. In the hour around sunset the blackbirds will "chatter" excitedly, a series of seemingly demanding repeated rapid calls that can dominate a park or garden at dusk. This may be four of five blackbirds or perhaps many more, all furiously chit chattering away. It seems like a blackbird competition to see who can be the nosiest bird, with no let up until suddenly the squabble ends as the last light fades and darkness, with silence, descends.

Seen where and when	Widespread everywhere, all year round
What it eats	Worms, insects, fruits and berries
Collective noun	A "cloud" of blackbirds, though only rare winter flocks
Lifespan	3-4 years on average, up to 15
Wingspan	14 inches or 35 cm
Length	10 inches or 25 cm
Latin name	*Turdus merula*
Alternative name	The Merle or Golden Bill
Also look out for	Thrushes, Robins and Starlings

The Chatterbox

The Goldfinch

Many birds choose to flock together and form tightknit groups. Some birds will form flocks that stay together for much of the year and others form flocks only during the autumn and winter months before breaking up again in the spring to form more independent breeding pairs. Birds may flock together for many different reasons, perhaps for protection from predators, to breed or to share a specific habitat or food source.

We often give particular flocks of birds their own specific name. These names tend to sum up the character of that flock and so we see a "gaggle" of geese, a "parliament" of crows and a "screech" of gulls.

All flocks of finches are delightful congregations and it is a joy to see gatherings of greenfinches and chaffinches rolling across the fields and cascading down the hedgerows. Perhaps the most enchanting finch of all is the beautiful little goldfinch, known in a flock as a "charm".

One of our smallest and yet most colourful birds, these fancy finches boast a bright red face and vivid yellow stripes across the length of their wings. They rove around in these bustling charms, searching out weed seeds or small insects. Not only do they look spectacular, they also twitter away to one another with a delightful twinkling chatter, a curious chorus of tiny tuneful bells.

Seen where and when	Gardens and open countryside, likes untidy areas
What it eats	Insects and weed seeds
Collective noun	A "Charm" or for all finches a "Trembling"
Lifespan	2-3 years on average, up to 8
Wingspan	9 inches or 22 cm
Length	5 inches or 12 cm
Latin name	*Carduelis carduelis*
Alternative name	The Red Cap or King Harry
Also look out for	Chaffinches and Bullfinches

The Charmer

The Green Woodpecker

The green woodpecker is otherwise known as the "yaffle", due to his distinctive high pitched *yaaffllle* like call, which carries long distances over gardens and across the countryside.

This woodpecker is as we might expect a vivid lush green in colour, whereas the greater spotted and lesser spotted woodpeckers are both white and black with a spot of red on their head or breast. The lesser spotted woodpecker is a tiny bird, no bigger than a robin, and is sometimes called the "lesser pecker"!

Both the green woodpecker and the greater spotted woodpecker are fairly common, but we are as likely to hear a woodpecker as to see one. When we hear the classic rapid drumming of a woodpecker pecking away at the trunk of a tree then this is almost certainly the greater spotted woodpecker. The green woodpecker, despite his name, only rarely pecks away in this familiar fashion.

The green woodpecker, with a bright red back of the head, feeds happily across our parks and gardens. Much of the food that they seek out is to be found in short grass and very often in our own gardens, for the Yaffle feeds mainly upon ants. We see them hopping happily across our lawns, using their large beaks to dig around for ants, ants and more ants before pausing to perch on a low branch or flying off in an undulating bobbing flight while making their loud startled *yaaffllle* call.

Seen where and when	All year round and widespread, loves garden lawns
What it eats	Ants, grubs and beetles
Collective noun	A "descent" of woodpeckers
Lifespan	5-6 years, up to 8
Wingspan	20 inches or 50 cm
Length	13 inches or 33 cm
Latin name	*Picus viridis*
Alternative name	The Yaffle or Yaffingale
Also look out for	The Greater Spotted Woodpecker

The Yaffle

The Swallow

Our spring and summer visitors are here to breed. They travel thousands of miles to northern Europe to breed and to raising young chicks. Our springs and summers provide ideal conditions for the growth of insects, bugs, plants and seeds – supplying our visiting feathered friends with an abundance of food and the perfect mild warm climate for chicks to hatch and fledge and to then feed themselves and to strengthen and mature.

By late April our days are becoming longer and warmer and all of nature springs into life. Flowers bloom and trees slowly start to show the year's first new leaf. But the surest sign that spring is in full swing is the first sighting of a swallow. Our long warm days of summer can now be only weeks away.

Swallows have flown 5,000 or more miles from southern Africa. They will spend the spring and summer months flying fast and low, sweeping over our fields and lawns and only ever feeding "on the wing". They don't even land to drink, but scoop up beaks full of water as they swoop rapidly across the surface of a river, pond or lake. It's a swoop scoop.

The swallow family also includes the slightly smaller house martins, who lack the swallows long forked tail. Both birds have truly astonishing navigational skills and may return each spring to the exact same nesting site, tucked high under the eaves perhaps only a few feet from our bedroom windows.

Seen where and when	Widespread in rural areas from March to October
What it eats	Flies and other airborne insects
Collective noun	A "kettle" of swallows
Lifespan	3-4 years, up to 10
Wingspan	13 inches or 33 cm
Length	7 inches or 18 cm
Latin name	*Hirundo rustica*
Alternative name	The Barn or Chimney Swallow
Also look out for	Swifts and Hobbies (our smallest bird of prey)

The Bringer of Sun

The Swift

Swifts spend almost their lives on the wing, staying aloft for long months at a time, hoovering up airborne insects for mile after airborne mile. They even sleep on the wing, sometimes rising a mile high on warm thermals before dusk, to float in slumber across the heavenly night sky. Swifts only stop flying for a few short weeks a year, briefly settling to nest and feed their chicks.

You will see them on August evenings in rapid manic flocks, wheeling low above rooftops and screeching with delight as they feast on swarms of summer insects.

Swifts, as we might expect, are extremely fast and can reach speeds of 60 mph in level flight. Few birds are faster, although in a steep dive a stooping peregrine falcon will reach an astonishing 200mph, making the plummeting peregrine not just the fastest of all birds but the fastest animal on earth.

Swifts are also long distance travelers and may well fly more than a million miles in a lifetime. But the almost unbelievable thing about swifts is that the young swift fledgling will take to the skies in early summer and will not then land for two whole years! Only as a two year old bird does the swift land for the very first time, in order to nest and raise young. Flying and eating and sleeping continuously on the wing for two whole years, having migrated to Africa and back twice, without ever having touched the ground.

Seen where and when	Widespread but patchy, from April to August
What it eats	Flying insects
Collective noun	A "swoop" of swifts
Lifespan	8-9 years on average, up to 15
Wingspan	16 inches or 40 cm
Length	7 inches or 17 cm
Latin name	*Apus apus*
Alternative name	The Devil Screecher or Squealer
Also look out for	Swallows and House Martins

The Bird Who Sleeps in the Clouds

The Kestrel

The kestrel is the second most common of our birds of prey, after the buzzard, and has one particular distinctive characteristic that makes it instantly recognisable; the kestrel can hover like a helicopter.

The kestrel is of little danger to other birds, hunting small mammals such as voles and mice and also feeding on grasshoppers and worms. Patient and highly skilled hunters, kestrels hover in full view above areas where their prey may most likely be found in the long rough grass beneath.

The kestrel's head remains absolutely still as they hover. With their keen eyesight, far better than our own, they pinpoint tiny prey in the thick grass below. They then drop in stages for a closer look, then another even closer look and finally swoop down in a rapid vertical dive before gathering their prey between sharp talons and devouring the unfortunate creature on a nearby post or perch. The kestrel will need to catch at least two voles per day in order to survive and in late spring perhaps six or seven, if they have young to feed. As such a single kestrel might hunt down over a thousand voles a year.

We often see them hover-hunting above motorway embankments and road verges, these often being vole friendly areas of longer and rougher grass. In the winter months kestrels save energy by spending less time hovering; at this time of year you are more likely to see them on a static perch, high in a tree or on a telegraph pole or wire, studying in vivid detail every inch of ground below.

Seen where and when	Across open country and road verges, all year round
What it eats	Small mammals, usually voles and mice
Collective noun	A "hover" of kestrels
Lifespan	7-8 years on average, up to 15
Wingspan	28 inches or 75 cm
Length	14 inches or 36 cm
Latin name	*Falco tinnunculus*
Alternative name	The Windhover or Mouse Falcon
Also look out for	Buzzards and Sparrowhawks

The Helicopter Bird

The Buzzard

Whereas the keen eyed kestrel preys on tiny voles the buzzard is hunting larger prey, most likely rabbits, preferably dead rabbits. Buzzard fly sky high above the fields and hills and yet still pinpoint small morsels hundreds of feet below.

The buzzard needs incredible eyesight to hunt like this and being so high in the sky can soar and scan over very large areas. Their large wide wings mean that they glide and circle seemingly effortlessly, often rapidly gaining height on a summer thermal, rising higher and ever higher with some minutes between wing beats.

We'll often we see three or four of these large birds soaring and circling together. These are likely to be parents with their offspring, teaching the young birds how to fly and soar and to hunt with the least possible effort. Buzzards are unfussy about food and may target a frail live rabbit but are happier picking away like a vulture at small dead animal carcasses or "carrion".

Other birds, often crows and jackdaws, will angrily mob these much larger birds, chasing the buzzard away from their own breeding or feeding areas. The buzzard's call is an unmistakable long mewing whistle, carrying wistfully for miles across hills and open countryside.

Seen where and when	All year round across hills, woods and open countryside
What it eats	Rabbits and small mammals.
Collective noun	A "wake" of buzzards
Lifespan	8-10 years, up to 25 years
Wingspan	44 inches or 110 cm
Length	22 inches or 55 cm
Latin name	*Buteo buteo*
Alternative name	The Shriek or Blood Hawk
Also look out for	Sparrowhawks and Kestrels

The Sky High Hunter

The Barn Owl

Almost all birds make some noise in flight as the air is disturbed by fast moving wings. But the graceful barn owl is completely silent. Making no noise at all in flight is a significant advantage for barn owls given that they fly low and slow over open ground, patiently hunting almost entirely by sound.

The barn owl's hearing is ten times as good as our own and enables this ghost-like bird to float across the fields picking up the slightest rustle of a tiny vole below. This acute hearing allows the barn owl to hunt at night, as they do not need to see their prey, although they are often also seen at dusk or dawn. Only because they are themselves absolutely silent can they pick up the tiny whispers in the long grass below, free of any interference from their own noiseless flight.

Barn owls numbers have declined due to the loss of the rough grassland habitat that supports the healthy populations of voles that these magical birds require as their staple food source. They can all too easily starve during cold hard winters as the harsh weather reduces the vole population. They also struggle in wet weather; their clever feathers enable them to hunt in silence but do not repel water and as such barn owls need spells of dry weather in which to hunt and feed.

Barn owls can sometimes be heard snoring, a surprisingly loud snore. We will sometimes hear their cry through the darkness, a chilling loud nighttime *screeeech.*

Seen where and when	Across open countryside, all year round, at dusk
What it eats	Mice, rats and voles
Collective noun	A "parliament" of owls (barn owls usually seen alone)
Lifespan	3-4 years on average, up to 15
Wingspan	35 inches or 90 cm
Length	14 inches or 35 cm
Latin name	*Tyto alba*
Alternative name	The Screech Owl or Billy Wix
Also look out for	Tawny Owls (commonly heard at night)

The Ghost Bird

The Little Owl

There are five owls common to The British Isles. The most common is the tawny owl, then there are the rarer barn owls, long eared and short eared owls and the suitably named little owl. They are all distinctively different in their habits and appearance, but all share the classic large eyes and still, upright posture. And they can all turn their heads far enough around to see almost directly behind them.

Most of our owls are fairly large birds and other than the short-eared owl are nocturnal hunters, hunting mainly at night. The pint sized little owl is only 8 inches tall, slightly shorter than a blackbird and only half the size of a tawny owl. The too-whit-to-woo that we will often hear at night is the tawny owl, whereas the little owl calls with a much more modest whistle like *kieew*, a rare call most likely heard in the spring and early summer.

One of our most surprising looking birds, the little owl is usually seen at dawn or dusk but can sometimes be spotted in the middle of the day, skulking around our woods and hedgerows. The little owl has a bounding undulating flight, similar to a woodpecker's, seeming to bob up and down with each wing beat.

Spotting a little owl is a rare treat, but if you know where one has been spotted then you may see the bird again and again if you return to that same area. The little owl is small but brave and will not always fly away if disturbed. We may sometimes, if we are lucky, see them quite nearby.

Seen where and when	Across open countryside, all year round
What it eats	Insects and preferably beetles
Collective noun	A "wisdom" of owls
Lifespan	3-4 years on average, up to 10
Wingspan	22 inches or 56 cm
Length	8 inches or 20 cm
Latin name	*Athene noctua*
Alternative name	The Little Spotted Owl
Also look out for	All the larger owls!

H'owl 'ittle the little owl…?
Very little indeed!

The Puffin

The remarkable puffin, when nesting, moo's like a cow. The puffin's nest is unusual as well, being a small rabbit like burrow near the sea shore. So the colourful puffin moos like a cow and nests in a burrow like a rabbit!

These lovable birds are only seen on land in the spring and early summer when they come ashore to breed. They fly low over the water with their short powerful wings carrying them quickly between their feeding grounds and their spring time burrows. They spend the winter and autumn in small groups many miles out at sea.

Puffins are outstanding underwater swimmers, diving up to two hundred feet below the waves, using their wings to propel themselves rapidly through the water and steering with their feet. They will catch small fish or scoop up large beakfulls of nutritious sand eels, these being their favourite food. Sand eel numbers are unfortunately threatened in many areas, harmed by industrial fishing practices, with potentially disastrous consequences for the local puffin populations.

One of our most unusual looking birds they have large brightly coloured bills and black and white plumage that make them look like waiters in waistcoats, or a swimming, flying, mooing circus clown.

Seen where and when	April to August in coastal areas and colonies
What it eats	Small fish and sand eels
Collective noun	A "colony" or a "circus"
Lifespan	20 to 25 years on average, up to 30
Wingspan	55 cm or 22 inches
Length	12 inches or 30 cm
Latin name	*Fratercula artica*
Alternative name	The Sea Parrot or Tommy Noddy
Also look out for	Our other auks, the Guillemots and Razorbills

The Moo Cow Bird

The Arctic Tern

Bird migration is one of the true wonders of nature. Our visiting birds spend only part of the year in our fields and gardens, or dispersed across our seas and shores. Many of these birds travel thousands of miles but by far the longest migration of all is that undertaken by the plucky arctic tern.

While many are to be found further north in Iceland and Greenland, the British Isles support a summer population of 50,000 or more arctic terns. They breed and feed in our northern latitudes, making the most of our long summer days. The arctic tern then makes an epic journey south, to the Antarctic, swapping our winter for the long days of the Antarctic summer.

No other bird migrates from so far south to so far north and back again. They will typically fly more than 40,000 miles in a year, covering over a million miles in a lifetime. In benefiting from the long summers of both hemispheres this remarkable sun seeking traveller sees more hours of daylight in a year than any other animal on earth.

These terns will aggressively protect their breeding sites. They will dive bomb and violently peck at a fox or other predator that may be threatening their eggs or young chicks.

Where and when	Northern and Western coastal sites, April to September
Feeds on	Small fish, crabs and krill
Collective noun	A "committee" of terns
Lifespan	25-30 years on average, up to 35
Wingspan	28 inches or 70 cm
Length	14 inches or 36 cm
Latin name	*Sterna paradisaea*
Alternative name	The Sea Swallow or White Daw
Also look out for	Common Terns and Sandwich Terns

The Long Distance Traveller

The Gannet

Gannets are one of our largest and most dramatic seabirds. A gannet feeding frenzy is one of the great spectacles of our coasts and seas. We may see dozens or perhaps hundreds of birds feasting wing to wing on a shoal of silvery fish. Soaring high above they use their excellent eyesight to spot silvery flashes of fish deep below the waves.

Once fish are spotted the gannet will plummet down, plunging vertically before breaking the surface with a splash and disappearing deep below. They drop headfirst at 60 mph with wings pegged back, slicing into the water and continuing to surge down diving perhaps forty feet beneath the waves, pursuing their prey like a torpedo. Then up they go again to repeat the feat, as gannets love to eat and eat. Gannets are of course notoriously greedy!

Gannets have special noses that close tightly when under water and extra padding around their beaks, saving them from getting a sore head and a nose full of water as they plunge again and again headlong in to the sea.

They breed only at a small number sites forming huge noisy and tightknit colonies of tens of thousands of birds. The largest gannet colony in the world is found on The Bass Rock in the Firth of Forth, where up to 150,000 gannets mass together and in doing so in such numbers they seem to turn the dark rock white.

Seen where and when	All year round, mainly on Northern and Western coasts
What it eats	Sardines, young cod, mackerel and the occasional squid
Collective noun	A "plunging" of gannets
Lifespan	18-25 years on average, up to 35 years
Wingspan	80 inches or 200 cm
Length	38 inches or 95 cm
Latin name	*Morus Bassanus*
Alternative name	The Bass Goose or Gant
Also look out for	Cormorants and Shags

The Torpedo Bird

The Oystercatcher

The stylish oystercatcher is one of only very few birds capable of prying open a sturdy oyster, shucking apart the shell with their unusually strong bill. But they will only rarely these days enjoy this particular treat, native British oysters being much scarcer now than in the past. The handsome oystercatcher is much more likely to be found poking about along our sandy seashores feeding on cockles and mussels, and limpets and worms. A better name for the oystercatcher might be the cocklecatcher.

One of our most distinctive seashore birds and widespread along most of our coasts the *cocklecatcher* is a bird that we see in all seasons on all but the rockiest of shores. They are a large wader and quite happy, like all waders, to dabble around for hour after hour up to their knees in the shallows. They strut around in search of food, keeping their neat black and white body warm and dry while their long pink wading legs seem immune to the cold of the sea.

From autumn through to spring they form small friendly and tightknit flocks, busily feeding close to the water's edge or in the shallows, using their long orange bill to dig for worms or breaking open those cockles and mussels.

Oystercatchers sometimes mate for life. As such a breeding pair might stay together for twenty years. A number of our birds demonstrate this same lifetime loyalty, other examples being the ever faithful jackdaws, swans and puffins.

Seen where and when	All coastal areas and inland in the north, all year round
What it eats	Cockles, mussels, worms and limpets
Collective noun	A "parcel" of oystercatchers
Lifespan	12-15 years on average, up to 25 years
Wingspan	33 inches or 85 cm
Length	18 inches or 44 cm
Latin name	*Haematopus ostralegus*
Alternative name	The Sea Pie or Mussel-Picker
Also look out for	Avocets and Curlew

The Black and White Cockle Catcher

The Heron

When you spot a heron you might at first think that you are looking at a statue. For long minutes at a time this tall gangly bird will stand stock still, not moving an inch as he stands up to his knees in the cold water of the seashore or lake or river.

While standing absolutely still like this the heron's prey is unaware of the tall hunter towering over the shallows. His long neck is nearly as long as his long thin legs, surely the longest legs of any British bird. The heron has a long sharp and dagger-like yellow bill. A patient and persistent hunter the heron bides his time before suddenly and rapidly striking down beneath the surface to spear any small fish that has unknowingly swum into range, stabbing the prey with their sharp and pointed beak before gobbling down the unfortunate fish in one greedy gulp.

The grey heron is unmistakable in flight, lumbering low across the sky on long slow beats of its huge wings. They are sociable birds in the breeding season, nesting in noisy colonies, called heronries, often building their nests close together, high up in waterside trees.

The heron's call is a croaky *frank, frank, frank*. Along with the rooks and crows they must be amongst the very grumpiest and most impatient sounding of all our birds, flying off if disturbed with a loud and angry *schaaaaaarr, schaaaaaarr, schaaaaaarr*. The unmistakable compliant of the unhappy heron.

Seen where and when	All year round in the shallows of rivers, lakes and sea
What it eats	Fish, small mammals and amphibians
Collective noun	A "scattering" of herons
Lifespan	5-6 years, up to 20
Wingspan	70 inches or 180 cm
Length/height	39 inches or 100 cm
Latin name	*Ardea cinerea*
Alternative name	Frank! Or Hegrilskip
Also look out for	Ducks, Swans and Geese

Frank, the Statue Bird